P9-CQK-967

A Visit to
COSTA
RICA

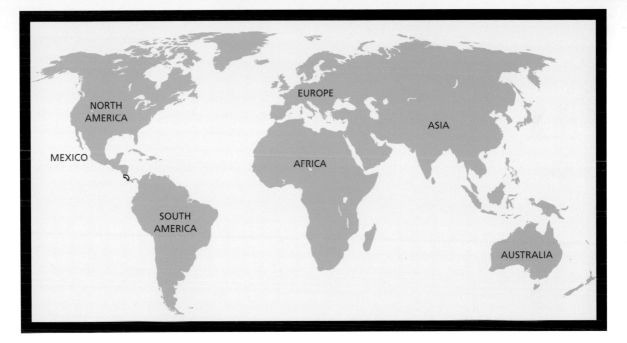

NORTH
AMERICA

MEXICO

SOUTH
AMERICA

EUROPE

ASIA

AFRICA

AUSTRALIA

Mary Virginia Fox

Heinemann Library
Chicago, Illinois

© 2001 Reed Educational & Professional Publishing
Published by Heinemann Library,
an imprint of Reed Educational & Professional Publishing,
100 N. LaSalle, Suite 1010
Chicago, IL 60602
Customer Service 888-454-2279
Visit our website at www.heinemannlibrary.com

All rights reserved. No part of this publication may be reproduced or transmitted in any form or by any means, electronic
or mechanical, including photocopying, recording, taping, or any information storage and retrieval system, without
permission in writing from the publisher.

Designed by Sandy Newell
Printed in Hong Kong

05 04 03 02 01
10 9 8 7 6 5 4 3 2 1

Library of Congress Cataloging-in-Publication Data

Fox, Mary Virginia.
        Costa Rica / Mary Virginia Fox.
                p. cm. – (A visit to)
        Includes bibliographical references and index.
        Summary: An introduction to the land, culture, and people of Costa Rica.
        ISBN 1-57572-379-4 (library binding)
        1. Costa Rica—Description and travel—Juvenile literature. [1. Costa Rica.] I. Title. II. Series.

F1544.F69 2000
972.86—dc21
                                                        00-029548

Acknowledgments
The author and publishers are grateful to the following for permission to reproduce copyright material:
The publishers would like to thank the following for permission to reproduce photographs:
Corbis/Martin Rogers, pp. 5, 8, 10, 14, 17, 22, 23, 24, 26, 27; Corbis/Dave G. Houser, p. 6; Corbis/Michael and Patricia Fogden,
p. 9; Corbis/Gary Braasch, p. 11; Corbis/The Purcell Team, pp. 13, 20; Corbis/Kit Kittle, pp. 15, 21; Corbis/Tony Arruza, p. 19;
Corbis/Joel W. Rogers, p. 25; Corbis/Buddy Mays, p. 29; Tony Stone Images/Tom Benoit, p. 7; Stock,
Boston/PictureQuest/Barbara Alper, p. 12; Aurora/PictureQuest/Peter Essick, p. 16; Stock, Boston/PictureQuest/David J. Sams,
p.18; National Geographic Image Collection, p. 28

Cover photograph reproduced with permission of Corbis/Martin Rogers.

Every effort has been made to contact copyright holders of any material reproduced in this book. Any omissions will be
rectified in subsequent printings if notice is given to the publisher.

Some words are shown in bold, **like this.** You can find
out what they mean by looking in the glossary.

Contents

Costa Rica

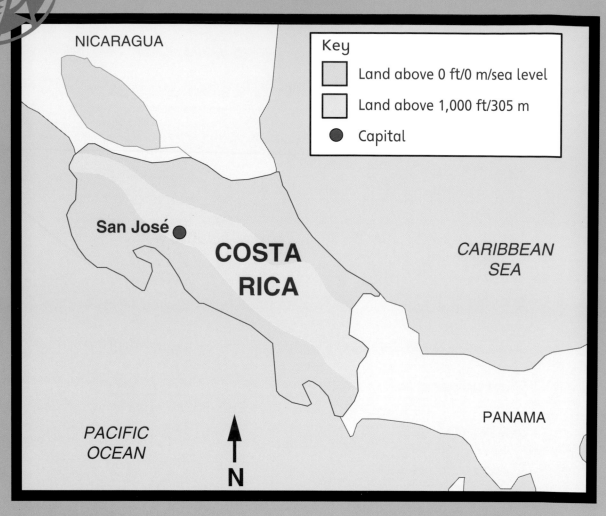

NICARAGUA

Key

Land above 0 ft/0 m/sea level

Land above 1,000 ft/305 m

● Capital

San José ●

COSTA RICA

CARIBBEAN SEA

PANAMA

PACIFIC OCEAN

N

Costa Rica is in **Central America**. It has one **coast** on the **Caribbean Sea** and one coast on the **Pacific Ocean**.

The name Costa Rica means "rich coast."
People in Costa Rica go to school and play
sports just like you do. Life in Costa Rica is
also **unique**.

Land

Costa Rica has low **plains** and **tropical rain forests** along both **coasts**. Here the weather is very warm.

In the middle of the country there are high mountains. Costa Rica also has **volcanoes**. They sometimes cover nearby homes and fields with ash.

Landmarks

The **capital** of Costa Rica is San José. The people of Costa Rica are proud of their beautiful churches. Some were built more than 300 years ago.

People from all over the world come to see the Monteverde cloud **rain forest**. Trees and plants grow on hills that are often covered by clouds. Many birds and animals live here.

Homes

In the middle of the country, houses are made of **concrete** blocks. They can stand up to storms and hurricanes. The houses are often painted bright colors.

Closer to the **coasts,** houses are often made of wood. They are built on **stilts** to keep them from flooding. In the cities, many people live in apartments or houses.

Food

Many fruits grow in Costa Rica. People like to eat bananas and mangoes. They also eat melons, oranges, and pineapples.

Red and white beans mixed with rice,
onions, and **spices** are a favorite food.
Soups and stews made with meat,
vegetables, and rice are also popular.

Clothes

Many children and adults wear jeans or shorts and T-shirts. Children in some schools wear uniforms.

For special celebrations, some women and
girls wear full skirts and ruffled blouses.
Men often wear straw hats shaped like
cowboy hats.

Work

Corn and coffee are two crops that are grown in Costa Rica. Workers pick coffee berries by hand. There are coffee beans inside the berries.

There are many factories in Costa Rica.
Some are for packing fruits and vegetables.
Other factories make instant coffee. These
products are also sold in other countries.

Transportation

In the cities, many people drive cars. On country roads, people often ride horses. **Oxen** pull carts that carry heavy farm loads.

There is a railroad so farmers can bring
their crops to ocean **ports.** A long highway
connects Costa Rica with other countries in
Central America.

Language

In Costa Rica, most people speak Spanish. This is because Costa Rica was **settled** by people from Spain. Many people also speak English. Often, words from both languages are used together.

When Costa Ricans go inside someone's house, they might say, *"Con permiso."* This is a way of asking permission to go in. Some people call each other *mi amor*. It means "my love." It is a friendly form of greeting.

School

Children start school when they are five years old. They study Spanish and English, math, science, music, religion, and art. Some children eat their lunches in the classroom.

The school year begins in March and ends in November. There is a two-week vacation in July.

Soccer is a very popular game. In Costa Rica, it is called football. Horseback riding is a sport and a way to get around. Races are sometimes held between villages.

Many places in Costa Rica are near the
water. People go to Costa Rica for **surfing**.
They also raft and **kayak** in the rivers.

Celebrations

There are many **fiestas** and fairs during the year. On October 12, people celebrate the day Christopher Columbus arrived in America. This holiday is called *El día de la raza*.

Many people in Costa Rica are Roman Catholic, so religious holidays are very important. Some holidays celebrate special people called saints.

The Arts

The native people of Costa Rica left many kinds of art. There are huge balls that were carved from stone. Other people carved beautiful statues with a stone called jade.

Art doesn't always have to be shown in museums. Some people in Costa Rica like to make everyday things into works of art.

Fact File

Name	The Republic of Costa Rica is the country's full name.
Capital	The capital of the country is San José.
People	People who live in Costa Rica are called "Ticos."
Language	Most people in Costa Rica speak Spanish.
Population	There are about four million people living in Costa Rica.
Money	The money in Costa Rica is called the colón.
Religion	Most people belong to the Roman Catholic Church.
Products	Crops such as sugarcane, coffee, bananas, and pineapples are sold to other countries. Clothes and shoes are made in Costa Rica, along with some small electric appliances.

Words You Can Learn

adiós (ah-dee-OS)	goodbye
maje (MAH-hay)	buddy, pal
pura vida (POO-ra VEE-dah)	okay
sí (see)	yes
gracias (GRAH-see-yahs)	thank you
buenos días (BWAY-nohs DEE-yahs)	good morning
buenas noches (BWAY-nahs NOH-chez)	good night
con permiso (cohn pair-MEE-so)	May I?
mi amor (mee ah-MOHR)	my love

Glossary

capital	important city where the government is based
Caribbean Sea	sea south of Florida that is part of the Atlantic Ocean and that is near Central and South America
Central America	land between Panama and Mexico
coast	land at the edge of an ocean
concrete	manufactured stone used to make buildings
fiesta	holiday fair or party
kayak	small boat with one long paddle that is used at both ends
ox	(More than one are called oxen.) large animal that is very strong
Pacific Ocean	largest ocean in the world
plain	flat land often covered in grass or small bushes that is used for farming
port	place where boats can stay
rain forest	deep woods with tall trees where rain often falls
settled	moved from one country to live in another country
spice	dried, ground-up plant used to flavor foods
stilt	long pole sometimes used to hold up houses
surfing	riding the waves on a special board
tropical	hot and wet
unique	different in a special way
volcano	mountain that has been formed by hot rocks pushing up through the ground and that can blow out hot smoke or fire and ashes

Index

More Books to Read

An older reader can help you with these books:

Haynes, Tricia. *Costa Rica*. Broomall, Penn.: Chelsea House
   Publishers, 1999.

Moritz, Patricia M. *Costa Rica*. Vero Beach, Fla.: Rourke
   Corporation, 1998.

West, Tracey. *Costa Rica*. Minneapolis: Lerner Publishing Group,
   1999.